WHAT AND WHO

Also by C.H. Sisson from Carcanet

POETRY
Selected Poems
Collected Poems
God Bless Karl Marx!
Antidotes

PROSE
Christopher Homm (novel)
The Avoidance of Literature
English Poetry 1900-1950
On the Look-out (autobiography)
In Two Minds: guesses at other writers
English Perspectives: essays on liberty and government
Is There a Church of England?

TRANSLATIONS
Lucretius, *Poem on Nature*
Virgil, *The Aeneid*
The Song of Roland

EDITIONS
The English Sermon 1650-1750
Christina Rossetti, *Selected Poems*
Jonathan Swift, *Selected Poems*
Jeremy Taylor, *Selected Writings*

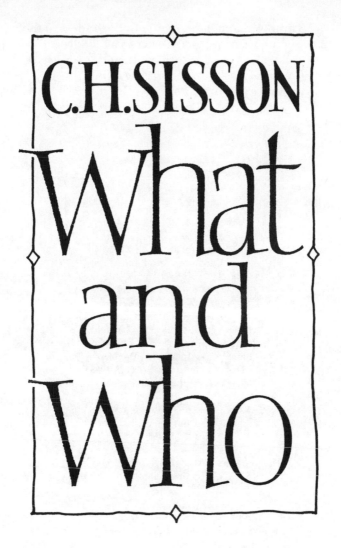

C.H. SISSON

What and Who

CARCANET

Acknowledgements are due to the editors of the
following publications: *Acumen, Agenda, Bostonia* (Boston),
Grand Street (New York), *Janus* (Vancouver), *London Magazine,
London Review of Books, New Criterion* (New York), *Outposts,
Partisan Review* (Boston), *Poetry* (Chicago), *Poetry Durham,
PN Review, Poetry Wales, Spectator.*

First published in 1994 by
Carcanet Press Limited
208-212 Corn Exchange Buildings
Manchester M4 3BQ

A CIP catalogue record for this book
is available from the British Library.
ISBN 1 85754 068 9

The publisher acknowledges financial assistance
from the Arts Council of Great Britain

Set in 10pt Palatino by Bryan Williamson, Frome
Printed and bound in England by SRP Ltd, Exeter

Contents

The Mendips

The stream that runs
Under the earth and is the stream of death
Is also that of life: without
Its sombre, unheard flow
What pulse would beat here or what ghost
Re-visit? Where
The sparkling shapes come tumbling from the mouth
Of that dark cave into the light of day,
The living are, and see
The splash and laughter of their ecstasy:
No sound. Imagination only made
That single figure dancing in the shade,
Naked as air, and it is she who slides
Into the mind and eats the heart away.
Turn back the spring
Which feeds the torrent: let the stream flow back.
The falling water mounts and disappears
Into the cave-mouth. All is quiet now.
The eaten heart goes with it, and the man,
Empty of grief as hope,
Watches the sunlight on the glinting rocks,
The tufts of bracken and the scattered flocks
Upon the hill-side. Age has come again,
And found its victim patient and at ease
Upon a world that has no power to please.

The Wind

The wind is rising, and it takes me past
Houses and gardens. Do I have a face
Any would recognise in this known place?
Is knowledge possible to be held fast
Either by me the merest breath can lift
Or the familiars who see me drift?

They still may know the living world, but I
Am perhaps not perceptible, or seem
Less than the emanation of a dream,
Recent but lost already in a sky
Too blank for definition, which is what
The others see who think of what is not.

I who look inwards see that nothing now:
They who look outward see me as I am.
This common truth, that leaves no room for sham,
Rejoices nobody, and that is how
Life ends, whose days promised us all, at first,
More than is found within the last and worst.

Et in Arcadia ego

And in Arcadia never have I, Charles Sisson,
Passed a day, my days have been otherwise:
I am the old Adam, in another garden,
Driven by tormenting angels from my prize.

The living days are over, and I remember
Only where I have failed, as any might,
On this or that occasion, with him or her,
When almost could perhaps have turned to quite.

So ends a journey which was hardly necessary,
Or so it seems, but what is done is done:
Fact has replaced illusion and I see
With what ineptitude the course was run.

Steps to the Temple

What is belief? A recognition?
Who knows of what? If any say
He knows, he lies.
Who knows what never was begun
And will not end? God is a way,
And a surprise.

And in that way we cannot choose,
For choice deceives us, as it must.
We live in sense,
Certain at least that we shall lose
That urgency, for we are dust.
Our recompense,

If any, cannot be to find
That beauty and that bitterness
Again. A new
Perception must await the vanished mind
– Or none, and which of these we cannot guess.
That much is true.

So here, we who are fallible
As shifting sands, may feel the tide
Flow over us, or in, or out.
If in, then all will then be well;
If not, then we should feel no pride
Even in doubt.

I talk from distant ti ies

I talk from distant times,
An empty voice, perhaps,
Or perhaps not. The past
Moves as the sun climbs,
Shadowing the present, maps
The future to the last.

None can escape its goad,
Boast though he will
Of the new light he bears.
He did not choose the road,
And travels still
With the familiar cares.

The contents of the skin
Contain all mystery.
Dress as you will, the mind
Sums all that is within,
And neither he nor she
Knows more than flesh can find.

Yet what it seeks is more
Than words can ever say:
All words that ever were
Haunt all that ever pour
From the dumb lips today
Of every him and her.

The two, who seek to eat
Each other, never can
Consume their prey, or speak
The hope that would complete
The woman or the man,
And therefore flesh is weak.

Language is all a lie,
And every utterance
Always extravagant.
Do not presume to try
More than the gift of chance:
The only word is Want.

Holà

Words do not hold the thing they say:
Say as you will, the thing escapes
Loose in the air, or in the shapes
Which struggle still before the eyes.
Holà will run upon its way
And never catch up with its prize.

Three Sonnets

from the French of Jean-Baptiste Chassignet

1

When old age enters we are well repaid
For the excesses of our youth; from one
Hearing, and from another strength, has gone.
The fittest stumble, by their eyes betrayed.

Our senses, each in turn, begin to fade,
Except the sense of desolation:
Disease grows stronger as the time goes on.
What a poor coffinful the corpse has made!

There is no part of us inhuman Fate
Does not mark as its own before due date,
Knowing that we grow weaker all the way.

Enough, everything dies in us but vice
Which, subject to a greedy avarice,
Living on death, grows younger every day.

2

Make sure you stifle your concupiscence,
Tearing the world's temptations from your heart,
But choosing your own moment to depart
Is something for which you are without God's licence.

The Christian leaves his earthly residence
When his due time is up: to flee in fear
From this pained body before the time is here
Offends the God to whom we owe obedience.

You must not hate your days too much, nor yet
Love them too much, for always there is set,
For one and the other, an appointed day.

God has determined that we are to fight
Here in the body till he sends the night:
The chief commands, the soldier must obey.

3
O great, amazing, strange affection
Of our Redeemer, whose avenging death
Not only saves our souls while we have breath
But saves the body for resurrection.

Formerly corruptible, in incorruption
It will live again; although sown in weakness,
It will rise again in vigour and in prowess
To live in glory, rescued from confusion.

Made in an animal body, it lives again
In a spiritual body, not serving men
But for the Lord, glorifying his name.

So life is alive and death itself dies
Because the second Adam bought this prize
And it was for this vivification he came.

Esperance

Meaning is what is lacking. Size
And shape are nothing in this room
Where there is neither light nor dark.
The usual servitude of eyes
Condemned to see the world in bloom
Is lifted, and it leaves no mark.

'Was somewhere once' is all there is,
Yet cannot be because it was,
By that precluding presence now,
For, in the last analysis
The past is only there because
The present lives to show it how.

This loss is more than all. I brood
On nothing but the vacant hour
Which slips away unregistered.
Language, be still. Do not allude
To any comfort in time's power:
Imagery has become absurd.

Yet there is spring, which breaks upon
The world without the help of man,
Subduing every living thing.
No emptiness can settle on
The mind it speaks to. Nothing can
Avert the meaning it will bring.

And though it seems that I must live
Beyond communication now
Of any wilful word or sign,
It needs only beauty to give
The light she cannot disallow
And every certitude is mine.

The Trade

The language fades. The noise is more
Than ever it has been before,
But all the words grow pale and thin
For lack of sense has done them in.

What wonder, when it is for pay
Millions are spoken every day?
It is the number, not the sense
That brings the speakers pounds and pence.

The words are stretched across the air
Vast distances from here to there,
Or there to here: it does not matter
So long as there is media chatter.

Turn up the sound and let there be
No talking between you and me:
What passes now for human speech
Must come from somewhere out of reach.

Explaining

All we can build is built on love
And everything we de-construct
Is merely an attempt to prove
That every flower is better plucked

BY US – professors, Ph.D.s,
And all who think intelligence
Cannot be shown by those who please
Only by holy negligence,

As, growing on a bank, or finding
A word by accident, and being
Indifferent to computer-minding,
Preferring hearing, smelling, seeing

The evidences of creation
To human ingenuity,
Convinced that any explanation
Is somehow less than what we see.

On living rather long

What wind blows now? For all is still,
Yet somewhere, certainly, a breeze
Assaults the summit of some hill
And carries foliage from the trees
While I, whom nothing now can please
Accept my stationary position
And cannot change my own condition.

Youth is a time when an event
Is bound to happen or impend
Without our knowing what is meant,
And ignorance is then our friend,
Giving us hope that, in the end,
Either we move on to despair
Or learn to relish the hot air.

And middle age is for design:
We think we know what we are doing
And where it's best to draw the line,
Content that we are not renewing
The follies of our youth, pursuing
The good we know until we find
That it was only in the mind.

We stand impeccably aloof
At last, and see the empty plate:
The eating was the only proof
The pudding could excogitate
– And that will always be too late
For hungry men, and when they're full
They find the appetite grows dull.

So listen for the wind, without
Asking what quarter of the sky
It comes from, what it is about,
Or either how it blows, or why.
It blows. However hard you try
You cannot mitigate its force,
Still less deflect its final course.

'Time: half-past nine, morning,' Wilfred Sisson,
Born to doom on the 13th, a Sunday;
The month was July, the year 1878:
I only perhaps remember him now.
Unravel yourself, past, and tell how
One born so early is remembered so late.
He had no son or daughter when he went away,
And it is only I who am bound to listen.

To me he is still audible. But regretting what?
I cannot decipher anything he said
Except this recording of his first moment
– Particulars he cannot have been aware of
When he crept into the world and found love
Not as reported, perhaps, for he went
Early to take his place among the dead,
Wilfully, as it is thought, rightly or not.

Vague ghost, who left no trace, except these:
Second-hand copies of a number of poets,
Not those of the moment or only of his century,
But Herrick, Wither, and several Mermaid dramatists:
These are the relics by which his spirit exists
And by which he spoke so unmistakably.
He could not evade the musical voice which sets
Beauty in the mind more painfully than prose.

That was his secret, rather than possible suicide
Or other adventure beyond which was thought licit.
The ancestral voice touched him. He recovered old furniture,
His great-grandfather's desk, and on the fly leaf
Of his grandfather's gardening book wrote his brief
Farewell, may be while he was still unsure
What his life would be or how he would take leave of it,
And what stars ruled his coming he could not decide.

Anyway he died, I do not know how old
He was when he fell into his last error,
Or where he went to seek his only relief.
I who have lived nearly eighty years have found
Some way farther in spite of the trembling ground,
Not finding either any secure belief
And stalked as he was by unnameable terror,
Certain only as he was it could never be told.

Another candidate for recollection
Is Charles Worlock, surely from my mother's family,
For they farmed in Gloucestershire since who knows when
– Perhaps since Saxon times there on the marches –
And he embarked under the shining arches
Of North Star and Plough, 22, fair, 5ft. 10,
No further away than Bristol, for where he would see
The blaze instead of southern constellations.

He did not sail there for astronomy
But altogether against his better judgment:
The judgment was that of a judge.
The jewels he stole were bacon and potatoes.
His gaol report was bad, but when he put to sea,
Good: whether the waves and sky gave him contentment,
Or merely left him without an immediate grudge
As the hulk rolled and the stars fell and rose.

Once in the Antipodes his conduct was not impeccable.
I will not record the full roll of his crimes:
One was to make 'five pairs of boots on his own account,
Without permission.' Was he not a shoe-maker?
That, certainly, had been his trade in Bristol,
In what he had not then regarded as happy times,
As perhaps they seemed on the purgatorial mount
Where he slipped so often on his way to his Maker.

He married Ann Wilson, an alleged widow
And a fellow-felon, who escaped from her wash-tub
And 'pretended to be free' – another misdemeanour.
In '59 he was insolent at the man-pushed railway,
Perhaps pushing it himself. In '67, they say,
Pardoned, he did not reckon that he could rub
His record clean and, maybe, thought that his behaviour
Would not do in Gloucestershire,
So, free to return whence he came, he did not go.

Sonnet

I well remember what it was to be
On the outside of what I was inside,
An office where the competences tried
Were not those which came naturally to me.
I had no notion of the fantasy
Entertained by the colleagues at my side;
I had my own – a solitary pride
Which drew me to the well of poetry.

Now old, I wander still and lack the light
Others can see by; nearly but not quite
Is still what others read as my device
Which either, blind, I cannot read at all,
Or for a moment dazzles, and I fall
Outside the in or through the slippery ice.

April

Exactly: where the winter was
The spring has come: I see her now
In the fields, and as she goes
The flowers spring, nobody knows how.

The Traveller

I have come far through a strange country
Where dead trees stand above the yellowed grass.
That was not all I saw, for further off
Snatches of green showed through the emptiness.
Sometimes I touched a leaf or felt the warm
Skin of an animal beneath my palm.
Yet the abiding desert was my tutor.
Strange that the love of beauty should so end,
And all the radiant world:
I dissolve into ether and am gone.

The Lack

All is past that is not now:
How long ago it seems!
What was, when life was, is remote
Beyond the reach of dreams.

The life was in the wants we had,
And now what do we need?
Less every day. True riches are
In hope, intent and greed.

How we fared in that starving time
Is less than the starvation
Which gave the future all its worth
And negatived negation.

But now, we only lack the past,
And now is less than then,
Less even than the direst lack
Which will not come again.

Eppur si muove

1

People I have not known enter my head,
Clear a room for themselves, and sit down,
Knowing that I shall welcome them, and the living
Are not likely to intrude while they are there.
Why so? Is this then a cavern for the dead?
Has it become so because under the frown
Of death there is no hope or forgiving,
Or in the hope that all there is fair?

The kingdom of the dead is no farther
Away than the centre of my mind.
It is there that the vanished speak, some word they said
Lights up or darkens my own vacancy.
It matters little enough what ghosts are there,
There is always some pain or folly to find:
The folly is mine and not that of the dead,
Who nod together, and in their nodding agree.

2

I who no longer circulate
Where people think they think, or do,
Know there was never yet debate
Where either *pro* or *con* was true.

What statement ever was? What act
Rested on more than movement?
And, on the simple bread of fact,
Is butter an improvement?

3

We who seem to others not what we are
But what they think we are: we the old,
Plausible travellers who have come from far,
Remember others of whom strange tales were told.

So generations find no secrets out;
The traveller came from nowhere after all:
The bold advance of thought became a rout.
It is some time since Adam had his fall.

4

Where is God's image? Deep within the brain
Or in the form he took and we have too?
The brain is addled and the world talks on,
But to some purpose beauty still is seen
Striding by, unconscious of herself.
What purpose? For the movement of the world.
Forget all else, for still the world will move,
Whatever meaning we attach to it.

To a Garden Asleep

Sleep, garden, in your beauty now:
You may, nor fear a meddling hand
Will dare disturb a single leaf.
Be what you are, your time is brief:
Do not attempt to understand,
Or wonder when or why or how

This moment will disintegrate.
It is, and while it is, you are.
The day is windless, and it seems
To hold the present fast; our dreams
Vanish into a distant star
Insensitive to human fate.

Extended leaves and petals fit
Exactly into the still air,
And neither proffer nor refuse.
The quiet is complete. No clues
Suggest another time will dare
To force your beauty to submit.

Thinking of Politics

Land of my fathers, you escape me now
And yet I will in no wise let you go:
Let none imagine that I do not know
How little sight of you the times allow.
Yet you are there, and live, no matter how
The troubles which surround you seem to grow:
The steps of ancestors are always slow,
But always there behind the current row,
And always and already on the way:
They will be heard on the appropriate day.

The Rake's Progress

The continuity of man
From before birth till after death
Is necessary to his kind.
Either the womb contains the mind
Which carries on to the last breath
Or history never began.

The baby who at last appears
And drinks his mother with her milk
Is clad already in the past:
Spinning and weaving hands at last
Achieved his gown of sack or silk,
As voices made the words he hears.

And there is nothing that he sees
Which ages have not modified.
The very smile his mother wears
Reflects how she conceives her cares:
The terms, slightly transmogrified,
Have been in use for centuries.

The clever men of Babylon
Who had ideas about the stars,
The Christian Fathers who could prove
That everything was made by Love,
A world of condoms and of cars,
Have brought their contribution.

The mother thinks, the child imbibes,
Then talking comes and carries thought
A generation further still
Without much effort of the will:
Words have more meanings than are taught;
It is the outside speech describes.

The world is found by bumping heads,
But also by analysis.
So theory mixed with bumps will give
The best instruction how to live.
The child grows up and soon he is
Full of invented hopes and dreads.

Most likely he will have ideas
– New ones of course, they always are –
But those damned words will not allow
Him liberty to work out how
The world of sense stands off so far
And does not fit his panaceas.

Then love comes, and ideas go:
Imagination fills the gap.
The body takes its rightful place,
Conceptual as the human face,
And he no longer cares a rap
For an abstracted to and fro.

He shrinks into himself, a squid
That quickly disappears in sand:
He has become a universe
In case he should find something worse
Than the delight he has in hand,
From whom, however, all is hid.

She cannot share the loveliness
He sees, for what she sees is him,
And there is not a perfect trade
Between the offers they have made
Of concept, promise or of limb;
Each gropes alone for a caress.

Both trundle through the course of time
But shapes and shades are all I see,
And sounds that fall upon the ear
Are all the persons that I hear.
The ghost of others is in me;
My ghost sticks somewhere in bird-lime.

Or are you empty, world? The birds
Gathering in autumn, are alive
And twittering too. We may depart
With half a word upon our heart,
To climb and circle or to dive
And scatter like the words.

Peat

If I could only return to where I am
From where I have been or from the vague reaches
Passing imagination saw, but not I,
The darkness would softly occlude the sky
And all sound faint before the barn-owl's screeches
Or the cry of a solitary lamb.

The sum of everything would be the peat
Which runs cool and dark between my fingers.
It is night itself, a peaceful shower
Which not one minute falls, not for one hour,
But endures while consciousness lingers
And follows it into its final retreat.

A Storm

O rain and wind, O wind and rain,
I not interpret what you say
But understand as if I were
A talking element myself
That speaks more faintly with each hour.
Yet every word and all intent
Loses itself among the wind,
Denounced under a flattening rain:
Presumption disappears, as best
Becomes the lips which might have spoken.

Beside the River

Two figures on a river-bank:
A full-grown man, a child of three.
The river passes them, yet stands
For all its flow, as still as they.

River! Exact and noiseless time
Passes as you do, and the two
So fixed there now, are not the same
As when your surface caught their eye.

The river holds their gaze, but they
Flow away into emptiness.
Or where? Who knows? Or who can say?
It is not time, but they, who pass.

Trees in a Mist

The mist is so thin, the world stands still
Before my eyes: there is no vanishing.
Dead figures ape the live ones which before
Breathed and were blown about by wind or will.
The winter cold embraces everything:
Death is the country I must now explore,

Yet cannot, and my corpse is not among
The number that I count before my eyes
– Trees which another time will bud and fruit,
And do not wait for any season long,
Though time seems long under these hazy skies
And there are trees which perish at the root.

So plays the outer world with that within,
And maybe that within with that without
– Consciousness no more than an interface
Between the two, with roots under the skin
And in the natural objects round about,
Housed where it occupies no shred of space.

And as the body perishes and finds
Itself confounded by the world of sense
– Taste, scent and hearing joining touch and sight –
The mist comes and goes; the river winds
Into the darkness: can there be pretence
Where there is neither confidence nor light?

Figure

It is quite easy to imagine thought
In any animal, as in this sparrow
Hopping reflectively with his mouth full,
Or this blackbird who walks disdainfully,
And at a distance, clearly occupying
A different universe of discourse. We
Have thoughts as well as they, but we have words
To claim more for our thoughts than they deserve.
Men and women have shape and colour, yet
Their thoughts seem verbal custom more than shadows
Of movements they may make or ways they go.
But watch this girl who bends to pick a flower.
Her eyes lighten, blue as what they see;
Her arm stretches, and the fingers flutter;
Her foot arches, the sole presses the ground,
The leg braces, then folds as she kneels;
The thoughtful back and head conclude her purpose.
Thoughts without words: the word is an intruder,
So, when she rises, turns, and shows her flowers,
The whole says, *Look!* and the whole is seen.
Is there another thought beside that one?
Now add a word. O what word can conspire
Against this beauty to make it vanish?
Would not the perfect word corroborate
The whole appearance of the world, and leave
Reality intact of any discourse?
Back to the sparrow and the strutting black-bird,
And you who stand before me in your skin.

The Levels

Summer has come, with no comfort
Except the cattle munching as they think,
And green being green where they bow their heads.
The river runs low, emptying itself
As if the sky itself were going out,
Streaming to westwards as the evening falls.
When light comes again, what shall we see?
Only the ruin of this ancient land,
And hear no more the old authentic words.
Yet somehow out of silence truth is born,
Which nothing now can harbour but herself,
And so succession will make all things new.
Let autumn come, and winter fill the dykes.
Spring will succeed, and the incredible
Prove itself by the plenty that it yields.

Conversation

It is by answering one another
That we exist. How else? How else?
For none alone, without reply,
Can with conviction utter 'I',
And even talking to oneself
Has part in it of him and her.

A shower of persons patters down
Upon the cradle where the child
Lies without briefing till a splash
Bounces back, and in a flash
A watching face, thereby beguiled,
Reads in it either smile or frown.

So in illusion there begins
Such conversation as there is
Between all creatures of a kind.
The fallacy promotes a mind
Fitted to serve the purposes
Haunting beneath our several skins.

And truth? And truth! Find if you can
Its plain location, or the words
Which hold it steady and secure.
The end of purposes is sure,
But truth is like the flight of birds,
Above the head of man.

Portrait of the Artist

What then am I? How can I be
A person that is spoken to
As others are, to whom I speak?
It is the otherness I seek,
And find by looking. So, how you
Appear, is how you are to me.

Appear is, for whoever looks,
The only *is* there is. Not so
For the one who is looked at. *Is*
For that one is the precipice
He stands on. He can never know
Who stands, or what man wrote the books.

The Question

Can who be what or what be who?
The question is resolved in you,
Though not *by* you, for you will say
Your many thoughts get in the way:
You think and think and therefore are.

Before you take Descartes so far
Consider how it looks to me,
Who think you are because I see.
Admittedly I cannot prove
That what I see and whom I love
Are interchangeable and one.
Yet no consistent theory can
Displace the woman and the man,
So either must remain for other:
And what is one without the other?
A person? And what is a person
Except a metaphysical assertion?
I hesitate to make one so
Detached from everything I know.
If what I see and touch is true,
Then what I see and touch is you.

Broadmead Brook

O you haunting ghosts, I move towards you.
Could I go over these flooded plains
It would not be to any Paradise:
I came from none and I expect to find none;
It was a long journey, or so it seemed.
The scene changed, and thoughts went through my head,
But even the possibility of knowledge
– Never coveted – seemed no more than a slide
From one thing to another. First the child
Tasting the world, and finding that it hurt;
Then the youth, felled by the bolt of love,
Then labouring where the knowledge was acquired
In self-defence or else in mere ambition.
But late in time and after all deceits,
I came to stand beside Broadmead Brook
As in the very hollow of my hand.
A woman stood there who had been a child
Where in another century my mother
Had played and laboured. Now all was changed,
Yet Broadmead Brook flowed, exquisite woods
Marked her course, for in my fantasy
It was she guarded the bounding deer,
The rabbits and the partridges, and all
Who dare to dream, and be, of England still.

Into the Darkness

The woods have fallen and the countryside
Vanishes from the eyes which knew it best.
What love was that which sought alternately
The open moorland and the crowding trees?
Do *they* make love, or does the watching eye
Merely have work to do for what within
The skull, the heart, the very finger-tips
Aches for companionship and can find none
But what has beauty for a name, and kindness?
Sleep on: it is a dream. Nothing I see
Speaks to me; it is I who speak to it.
Yet words, we know, do not answer the call
Of inmost need, for that would mean reply,
And nothing speaks to me, for beauty is
A hunger, not a feast, and it is made
By wants we have and not by what we are given.
Fall, trees: I can do nothing for your growth.
Conceal yourself, beauty, before my eyes
Which bring you nothing but my hunger.
What I bring to the failing countryside
Is nothing but the failure of my need.
It is for youth and hope that morning breaks.

I who am

I who am and you who are
– If we are, as we suppose –
None the less are very far
From knowing what each other knows.

Even the curl of that curled leaf
Is not the same for both our eyes,
Much less a hope, much less a grief,
A memory, or a surmise.

Much less the whole that makes the Is
Of any living creature. I
May utter perfect sentences,
As so may you, who make reply,

But these toy structures are no more
Than any rule held in the hand,
And what your words, or mine, are for
Is not a thing we understand.

So ask the body. It alone
Knows all you know, and it imparts
Little enough of what is known
To what we call our minds and hearts.

So fumbling bodies try to make
Friendship and love as best they can:
None ever was without mistake
And lies by woman and by man.

Man lies by woman, woman lies
By man, and in a common bed.
Where is the rule which truly tries
What is done there by what is said?

On a Drawing

Toi à qui . . . You had never speech;
Only the lines on paper spoke.
No words of mine could ever reach
The silence that you never broke.

Beauty is poised in clear mid-air
And there you are, and there you stay:
For my cold words to find you there,
What silence must they not convey?

The poet and the work of art
Meet where the silence of the word
Encounters lines which have a part
In every echo that is heard.

And you who wore, and were, the flesh
These lines endeavour to translate,
Cannot yourself keep memory fresh
Of what was at that distant date.

It is abstracted lines that live,
While you must die, as others do;
A draughtsman, certainly, can give
A longer memory than you

– But not of you; the temperature
Of flesh, its movement and its thought,
Have no pretence here to endure,
Nor fleeting colour to be caught.

You see the lines the draughtsman drew
Although yourself unmade by time;
I see, and what I see is you
As others saw you in your prime

– Or so your presence is to me,
I boast, I think, I partly lie:
The poem holds you silently
And in that silence words must die.

The Mappemonde

The face, hardly issued from innocence,
Where walls of flesh held fast her feet and hands,
Is fresh as dew, and the emergent limbs,
Tiny at first, grope to achieve their shape.
She has the pulp and surface of a grape:
Do not crush her. It is a new life brims
In that soft skin before she understands,
Or senses congregate and so make sense.

Insensibly she grows, but sensibly
Takes in the size and meaning of those blocks
Of hard and soft, those loud and quiet things
Which make the world before the world begins.
Legs and arms do the work of tail and fins,
Propelling this small fish until she flings
Prudence aside, and first kneels, and then rocks
Upon unstable feet for all to see.

So is childhood begun, and consciousness
Grows like a weed within this harmless frame,
Tangled with others as it turns and twists.
You may, indeed, doubt how it can affect
The flesh in which it is rooted, or the aspect
Of that stripped form by which alone exists
All that can have a hope or bear a name.
Yet a face may be thoughtful, none the less,

And thought does not end there. The body flows
Through the slim torso, lengthening arms and legs
– And as they run, dive, frolic and be pleased,
Sayings all quickly seconded by the tongue,
Which speaks also for stomach, heart and lung
And every nerve demanding to be eased.
So every syllable the body begs
Is written in the skin from scalp to toes.

O words joined to the flesh, as once the Word,
And so when shoulders firm and arms grow round
And there is definition in the breasts.
Although the whole frame hesitates to be
The woman who took apples from the tree,
Yet time runs on, the time that never rests,
Until the first maturity is found,
The unmistakable Eve is seen and heard.

Even her smile is ambiguity;
The look and looked-at tumble in her brain
– The arms meant to assist or to entice,
The breasts are apples to the glancing eye,
The patch of hair below writes clearly why.
Yet the whole figure gives more sad advice,
That youth once lost will never come again:
The future comes, in which no one is free.

This was her mother not so long before,
Her mother and her mother, till the past
Runs into darkness. Soon, shaped like a pear,
Her body still resembles theirs, and out
Falls a small girl: the times have turned about,
But she goes, full sail, into different air:
See how her comfortable flesh at last
Rises and falls, breathing at every pore.

Then age. No body is comfortable
In that last scene. No softness of the skin
Can compensate for the receding tide,
Nor any kindness written on the face.
The arms have lost their stretch, the legs their pace.
Yet still only falsity can divide
The outer life from consciousness within,
And at the resurrection all is well.

If I were accused

If I were accused of what I have said
I could perhaps answer; I should at least
Have something to say which proposed meaning
– Reason enough for speaking, although the dead
Cannot avail themselves of it, and the beast,
Even while still living, finds its demeaning.

A roar or a bark or a miaow merely asserts
Existence and essence without saying why.
They are mysterious who cannot answer back.
So let nature reign; yet mystery may hurt
The Icarus who pretends that he can fly
Too stupendously close to the sun's track.

And so this girl, in whom the vanity
Of finished beauty may occlude sight,
And she see no more than she can say.
We are condemned to words: if what we see
Can never be discovered in more light
Than they can give, there is no brilliant day;

There is no brilliant object made to fill
Brimful the mind and leave no room for speech.
This girl herself will lose the wakeful shine
Of shaped and iridescent flesh, until
Whether she sit or stand, or run or walk,
Not she, but only words, can give a sign.

Adam, who named the beasts as they came by,
Had no name for the wonder that he felt,
But we have words to hide things from our eyes.
Read what is – the birds as they fly,
The lap of waters, snows as they melt.
Only a speechless look can be wise.

In the Silence

The silence of my days
Deepens, the wind is still:
Unbroken cloud or haze
Wraps up the world until
The minds which once seemed full
Seem empty, dark and dull.

I speak, and no one hears:
I listen, no one speaks.
There is no sound of tears,
No laughter. No one seeks
The future in the past
Where it must come at last.

And is the future new?
They say so, who ignore
Adam and Eve show through
Today as heretofore.
The murder done by Cain
Is daily done again.

Celebrate if you will
The triumph of your genes:
The past is working still
– That is all that it means.
In every spoken word,
Always, the past is heard.

Perhaps silence is best,
But if there must be speech,
Then watch it closely, lest
It stretches out of reach.
The future is too far;
The past is all we are.

The Model

Certainly speech is not possible,
For what are words without the world that speaks?
Voices in air come from the solid earth.
Green fields speak of May and all is well:
It is the sea tells what the river seeks:
It is the sky which says what heaven is worth.

And so with touch and every other sense,
For what are hard and soft without a stone?
Or scent without the dunghill and the rose?
Fill up the world and you may recompense
The listener listening to the hollow tone
Of sounds without content, or mere prose.

But yet who speaks? There must be speakers too
And you may have encountered one, who touch
The strings they speak with and you listen for.
How designate the speaker, and what drew
You to that note you loved little or much?
It was the garment that the speaker wore.

What garment? If the speaker is within
It is none other than the flesh she wears,
Where all the voice holds may be touched and seen,
So what her speech carries will begin
To bear the timbre that the body bears;
The world will partly mean what she may mean.

All love is dangerous, but to regard
The body as it is, is what must be
If speech is to impart its share of truth
And carry sights and sounds, and soft and hard,
The non-numerical reality
Which billows round us into age, from youth.

The words we say are part of what we are:
All flesh is grass, and so is what we say.
Observe the people passing in the street:
The words they use come to them from afar;
The use is only what they are today,
And what they are is in the flesh complete.

And so I turn to you: the conversation
Is because you are, and I seek to know
How that frame ripples as your words come out.
Except as love and knowledge are the same,
It is not love but words I seek, and so
I hope no more than to be cleared of doubt.

The Rose

What the words carry and the things you say
Must be related, but the saying is you
And what the words carry is history
To which you add your infinitesimal day.
Sweet rose of England, nothing can be true
Except so far as words and you agree.

And how is that possible? My dear,
The tongue you speak must so become your tongue
That it becomes like kisses on your lips,
Given and received at once. Then, without fear,
Your diction answers to the clear line sung
By lutenists, which dips as the voice dips.

So, when words had the colour of the flesh,
And passed from mouth to mouth, and were not laid
Like corpses on a script or on a tape,
The fields rang with laughter, or the fresh
Cry of misfortune. Now speech is a trade,
The word congealed and all meanings escape.

Absence

Go back, or forward, to a time
When I am not here. What remains?
What is here is what I see,
For I trust visibility,
Find that I get wet when it rains
And think that sense and reason chime.

No sense, no reason. For the past,
The living stand in for the dead
And try to see what others saw,
Though disappearance is the law
For what is seen, and what is said,
Though cast in bronze, can never last.

And so one can imagine sand
Carried back by receding tides,
And yet not understand a word
The ocean said when it was heard.
The present never co-incides
With any past that comes to hand.

Go forward. I am here no more:
No word of mine can extricate
The listener from the cord that binds
Him in the twist of other minds.
Unheard before, and now too late,
My words have lost the flesh they wore.

I am not even silence, as
The rows on rows of marshalled dead
Who left no word they did not speak.
An echo that is faint and weak
Remembers me for what I said,
Happy to lose the man I was.

Casualty

It is not the spoken word but the word spoken
In silence, not directed at anyone,
But holding meaning till it spills over,
Which finds its way into the casual mind.
Poetry, ha? The bed-rock of that art
On which those few can build who lose themselves.

A Word in Time

If I knew what to say I would say it now,
But speech is at an end, the words you hear
Echo through empty halls of past decades.
Others may speak again, but not I
Who am forbidden by age and emptiness.
Those halls ring with what cannot be
Because it was, in another time.
Pass on, present, into futurity,
Leaving your husk of past for other teeth.
Who munches on that will never know
The light which falls this morning nor on whom
It falls. So, expect nothing from me
Who spoke of yesterday and what I saw,
Which now has vanished though the words remain:
The flesh has melted and the noun rings hollow.

The Pattern

The Pattern

The days seem long now, and life is long
Although the years hurry away to death;
No one can daunt time; the young and strong
Are weak before it draws their dying breath.

It races, and they race, and still they lose;
The beds they tumble in grow comfortless.
How could imagination ever choose,
Since out of more there comes always less?

The gangling bunch of nerves which reach the brain
From every corner of the fleshly kingdom
Collects the news of beauty, but the pain
Of memory will devour comfort's crumb.

What is remembered of the years at last
Is nothing but the folly of the wise,
Prudence too much, or too much folly past,
No calculation helps the man who dies.

What comes back is that every choice is wrong,
No action finished as it was conceived,
The body withered while the hope was strong;
No itch it suffered ever was relieved.

O mind, the frenzy of a fluttered nerve,
What did you see as you went on your way?
What do you see now? Nothing will serve
To mitigate the horror of that day

When all goes crumbling to its final end;
The end of ends was far before that time.
No purpose was achieved, nothing could lend
The colour of intention to the climb

From that first pulp which once within the womb
Lived as unknowing as the wisest man,
To reach that image-decorated room
Death wipes as clean as when he first began.

Yet the pulp rises like a loaf of bread,
The harbouring belly swells, and then ejects
A naked clown who falls upon his head;
His parents see, he does not see, his prospects.

The reason of the world is in those two,
The one that bore, the one that set the seed;
The child is what he must be, and what grew
Once in the dark, finds what it is to feed.

Before the eyes can focus, ears can hear;
A cloud of sound bursts on the sleeping brain:
Then forms take shape, hunger may come, or fear,
An ancient pattern growing once again.

Love flashes from the eyes that wear the paps;
The peace they give resembles gratitude.
What deceits on both sides! The love perhaps
Following the particle it must extrude,

The gratitude compelled by satisfaction
Unable to attribute its delight:
A blind cradle rocks, and the exaction
Returns the infant to his sacred night.

So from this darkness does this ignorant
Grow senselessly, a tree without a root,
Only his predecessors confident
These vague extensions are a hand or foot.

So words collect which have no meaning yet,
Like dross upon the brain in sucking-time;
Sights veer and cloud and are indefinite;
The child moves in the chaos of his prime.

Movement it is that brings definition,
The toe, the toy, the blow or else the fall.
Wisdom creeps in then like the Evil One
To advise how to bully and to call.

And so to play, and give to fantasy
Control of every monster in the way;
Mind like a platitude will always see
Itself victorious in the shining day.

And then to youth, certain and arrogant,
Or weak and frightened when it finds defeat,
Still groping with its stream of youthful cant
To find a proper use for hands and feet.

The feet which lead him to the proper prize,
The hands which seek for softness once again;
The conjugation mastered by the eyes
Inflecting what until it turns to when.

To climb upon the body that he chose,
Yet did not choose but willingly obeyed,
Those breasts, that belly, that imagined rose
Blooming under the bush which marks its glade.

The bed of love declares itself supreme,
Yet not the love but only the desire
Which finds its solace there, is the true dream
Throwing itself upon its funeral pyre,

That desire which must flicker and then blaze
So often in what seem long years ahead,
Twists itself into many shapes and plays
Far subtler games than any in a bed.

The conqueror is happy on his horse,
The politician revels in acclaim,
The petty thief approves his clever course:
The hope that drives their movements is the same.

Justification in the eyes of men:
The lies crowd around the winner and he laughs.
And when he fails, as he must fail? Ah, then
He lies to please himself, and laughs and laughs.

So the word grows upon a tree of nerves,
To deceive all who take it for the fruit.
What fruit is there? The dying body serves
At last to stultify it from the root.

It came first rather as a bird to perch,
Twittering perhaps upon an utmost twig:
The dying body leaves it in the lurch,
The structured growth solid and gaunt and big.

The twig has lost its sap, the word its meaning.
Can it fly after that? The flock that fell
Bird after bird from nowhere, and sat preening,
Rises no more, and has no news to tell.

A twitter here and there is taken up
By other birds, perched upon other trees:
Then silence: other mimics fill the cup
Of the surrounding world, and seek to please.

And other movements bustle and are lost,
Of other bodies moving as they must,
For no word suits them, and their hopes are crossed
As others were which now compose the dust.

If any came, it was the only Word
From the beginning and beyond the end:
It was made flesh – which you may think absurd –
And if it was not, no man has a friend.

What mind is that which floats above it all?
Histories happen, words float everywhere.
Can they find meaning? They swoop and fall,
Homing on scattered hope, scattered despair,

Where men and women clutch at anything
Which for a moment seems to promise mind:
Build then who can, and teach the voice to sing,
Help them all to resemble human-kind.

Build cities, where the busy man may hide
His hope under a heap of emptiness.
Child-birth under a roof will turn to pride:
The most presumptuous building is a dress

And those who enter it with clothes and names
Still seek the cover of a common garment;
No cloth so fine that it can hide their shames,
No tower so high that nothing more is meant.

O poverty of man, woman and child,
Wordless at first and seeking to conceal
The unconversible heart which runs wild,
The mind with shapeless thoughts, and none is real.

How can they sleep or die without dreams?
Much less move, walk here or there for reasons
They tell themselves: what is is not what seems;
Sleeping and waking, for all, feed on treasons.

Remove all cover, pull the building down,
Strip off the clothes, show up the naked pair:
They are not stripped enough by half, the frown,
The smile express their dream that they are fair.

The sad creation of their own conceit:
The words they learned carry the poison in,
False hopes and fantasies which they repeat
To the tune of the blood beneath the skin.

Strip off the words that they are pleasant with;
They mean what the blood says and nothing more.
The blood pumps on and they cannot forgive,
Later, the many lies they told before.

Strip off the flesh, which brought them to this pass,
And what is left? Ah, there the world is dumb.
How else does any see wind over the grass,
The flowers assailed, or hear the insects hum?

How else see blue sky and brilliant cloud,
The river passing and the swan at rest?
How speak of them and not cry aloud?
How praise what must be praised and loved best?

The words which fall like petals from the sky
Are all they have, and not as instrument,
Only as gift, which none may have who try
To turn these driftings to their own intent.

The body, yes, without it they are not,
Nothing can do and nothing understand.
The rasping mind pretends to have a thought:
It lies, and cannot even lift a hand.

The paradise of the Resurrection
Waits for its people, or else nothing is.
Choose you cannot, but, chosen, fall upon
Knees if you have them, and some certainties.